THE MUSIC TREE
CHRISTMAS

7 Duets for Student and Teacher

PART I

**Arranged by
Louise Goss
Sam Holland &
Steve Betts**

Contents

Alfred

O Come, All Ye Faithful
(Adeste Fideles)

Translated by Frederick Oakeley

Music by John Francis Wade

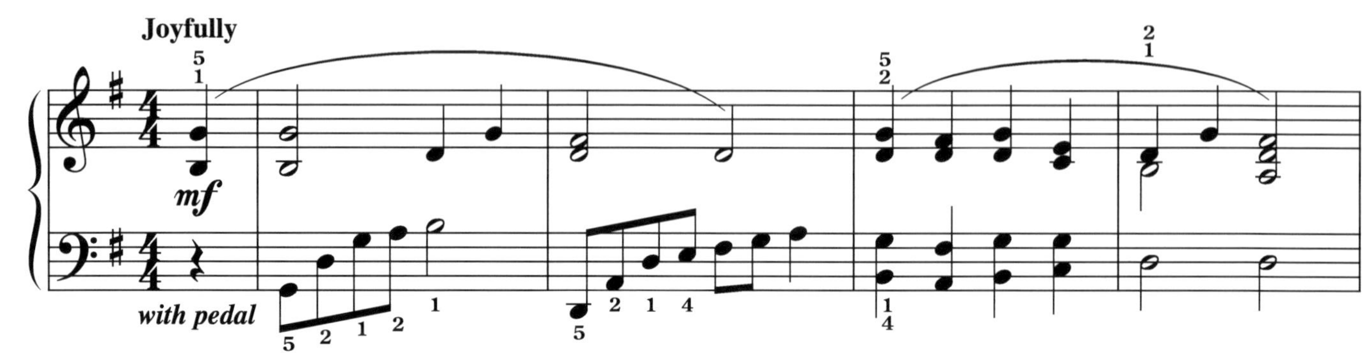

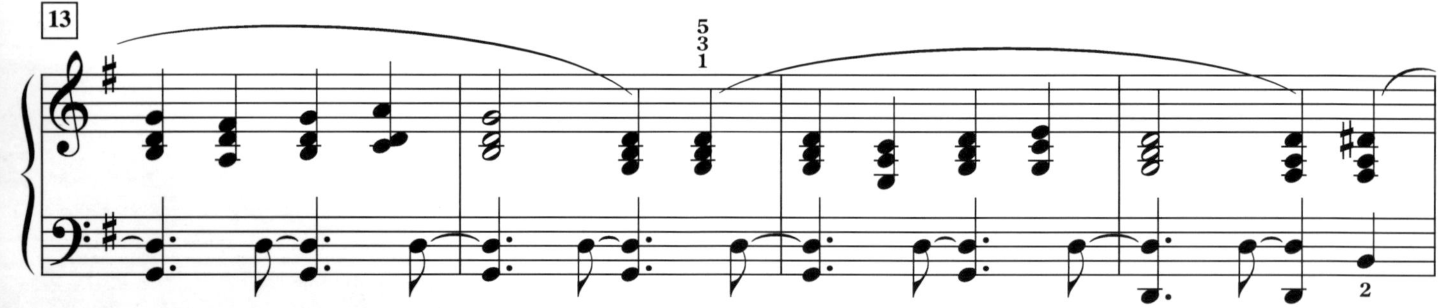

2

O Come, All Ye Faithful
(Adeste Fideles)

Translated by Frederick Oakeley

Music by John Francis Wade

It Came Upon the Midnight Clear

Words by Edmund H. Sears

Music by Richard Storrs Willis

It Came Upon the Midnight Clear

Words by Edmund H. Sears

Music by Richard Storrs Willis

Gloriously (*Two octaves higher with duet*)

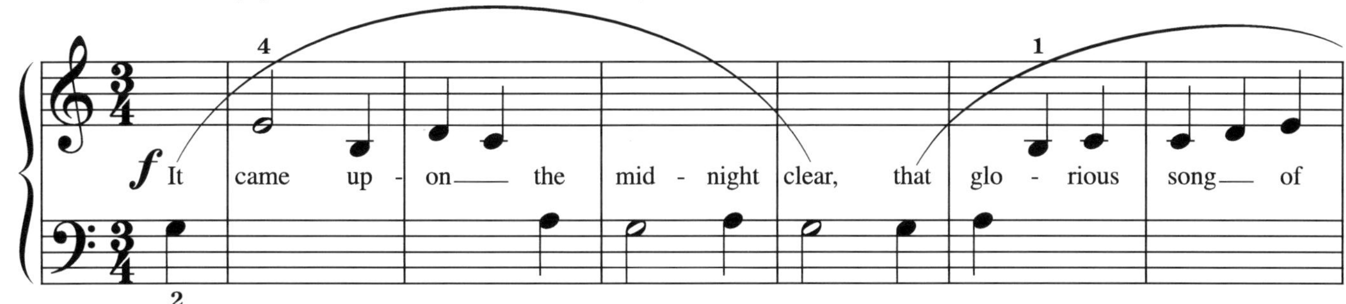

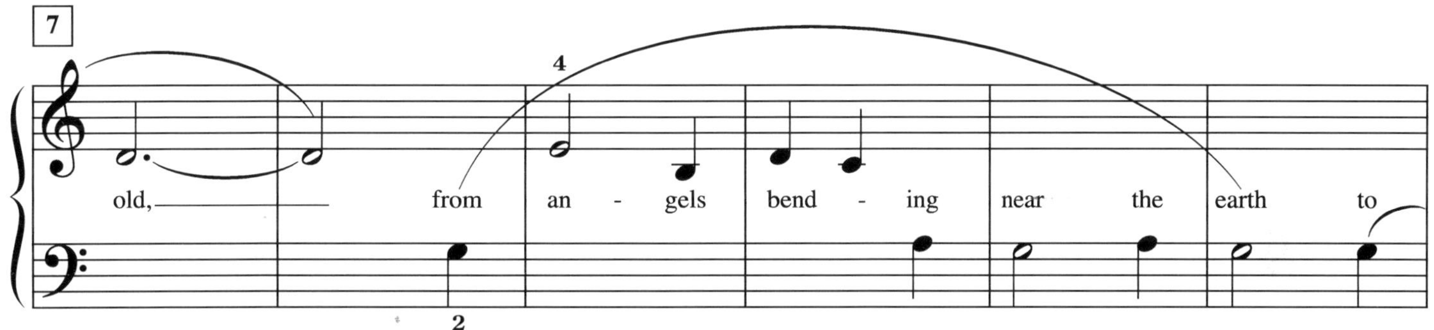

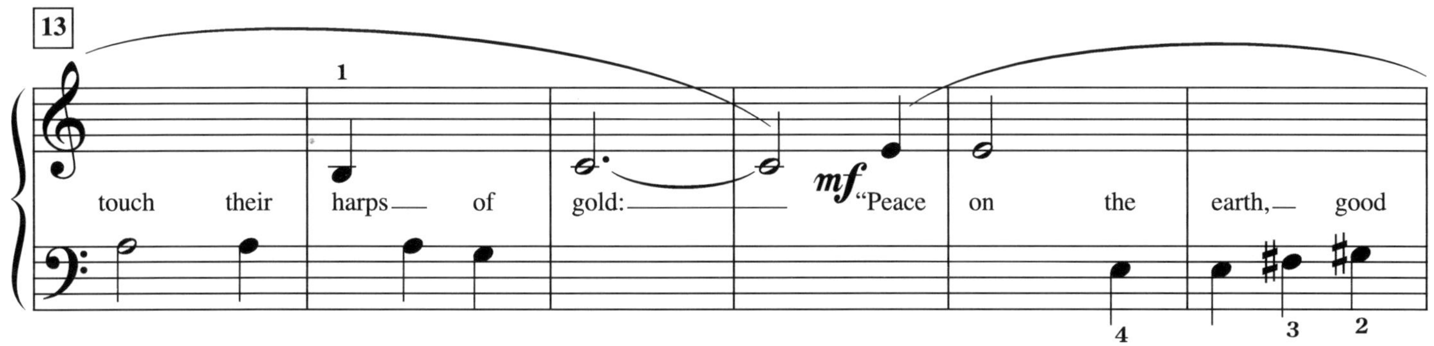

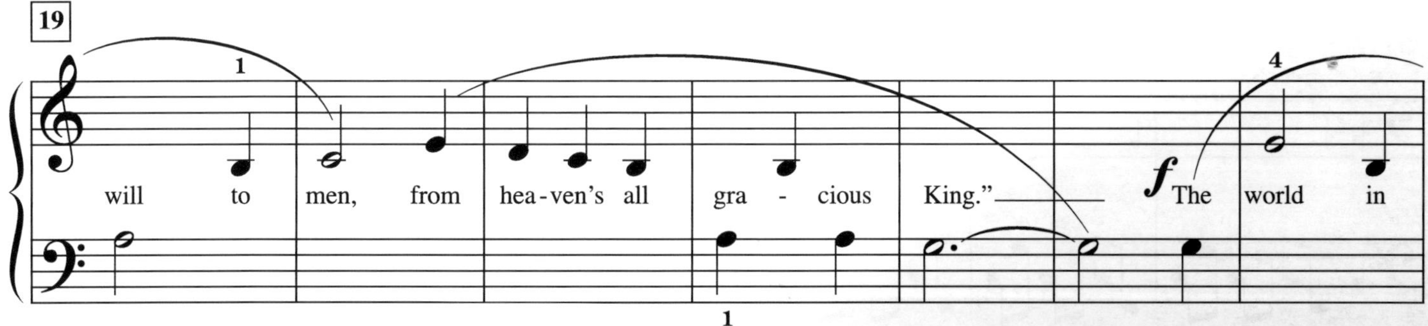

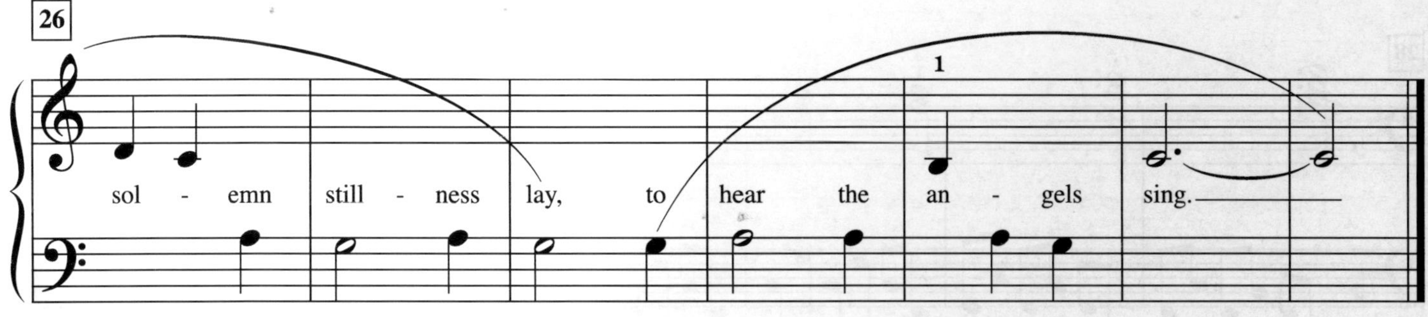

We Three Kings of Orient Are

Words and Music by
John Henry Hopkins, Jr.

We Three Kings of Orient Are

Words and Music by
John Henry Hopkins, Jr.

Good King Wenceslas

Words by John Mason Neale

Traditional

Good King Wenceslas

Words by John Mason Neale

Traditional

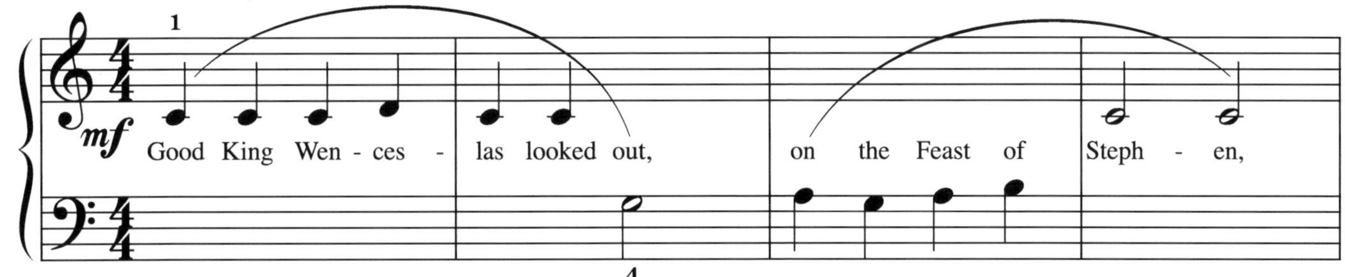

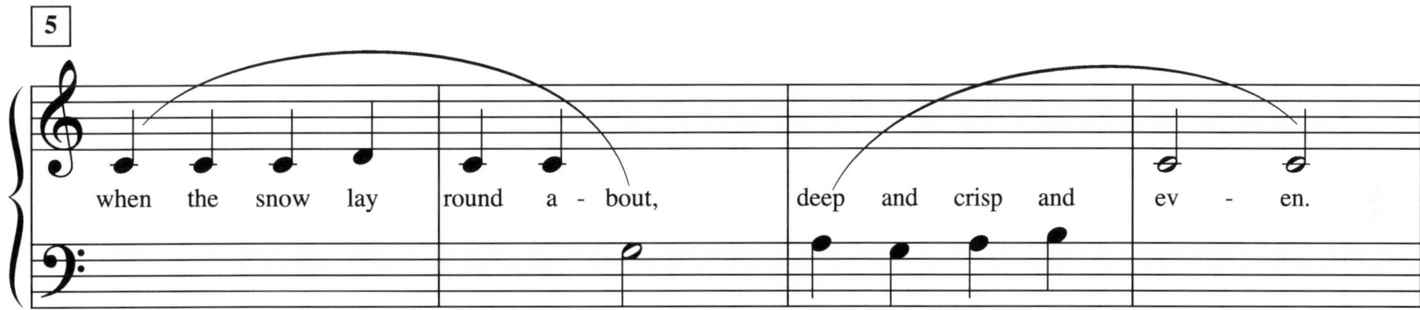

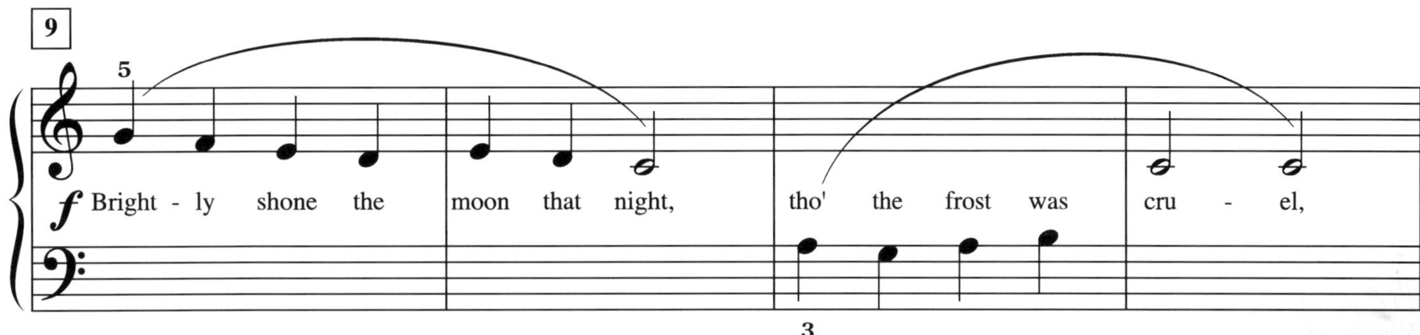

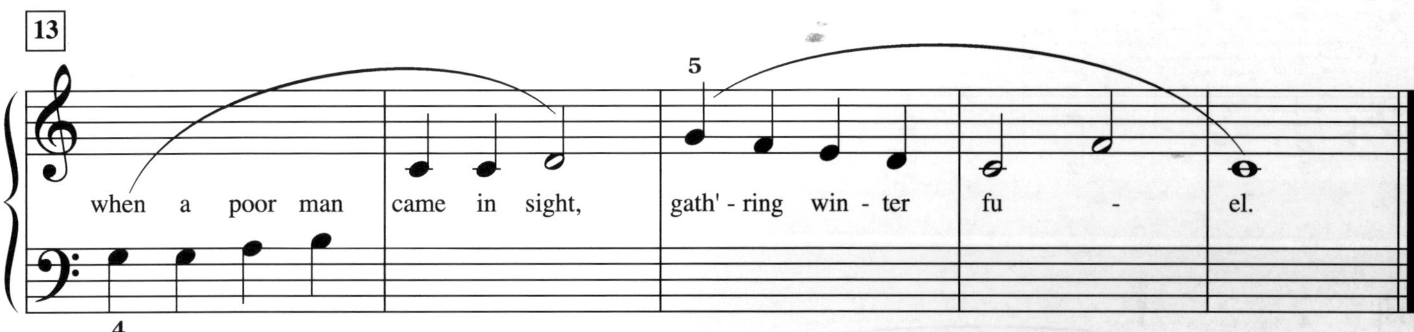

2. "Hither, page, and stand by me,
   If thou know'st it, telling,
   Yonder peasant, who is he?
   Where and what his dwelling?"
   "Sire, he lives a good league hence,
   Underneath the mountain;
   Right against the forest fence,
   By Saint Agnes' fountain."

3. "Bring me flesh, and bring me wine,
   Bring me pine logs hither:
   Thou and I will see him dine,
   When we bear them thither."
   Page and monarch, forth they went,
   Forth they went together;
   Thro' the rude wind's wild lament
   And the bitter weather.

Good Christian Men, Rejoice
(In Dulci Jubilo)

Translated by John Mason Neale

German Carol

Good Christian Men, Rejoice
(In Dulci Jubilo)

Translated by John Mason Neale

German Carol

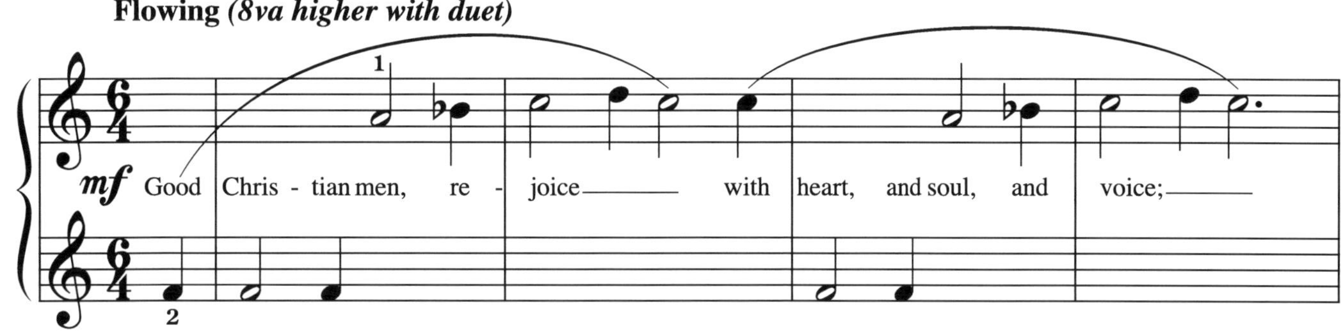

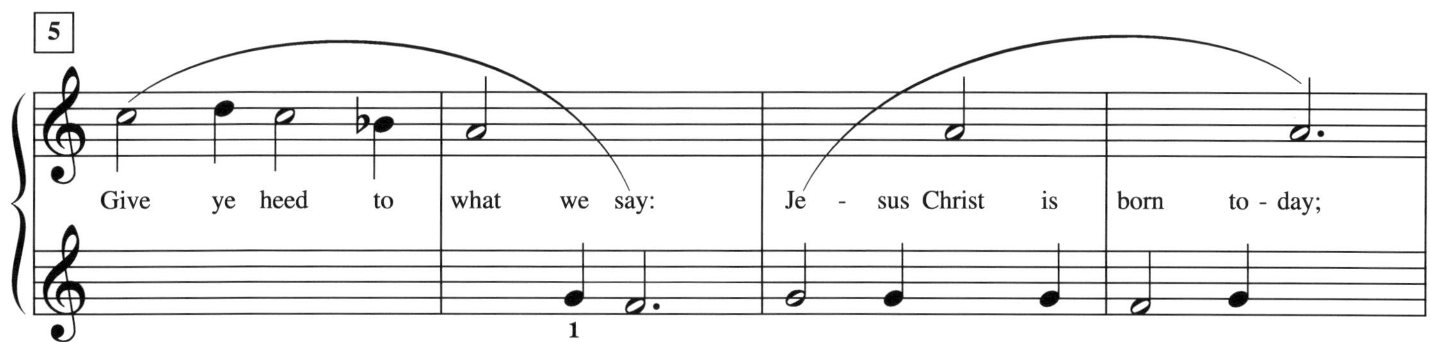

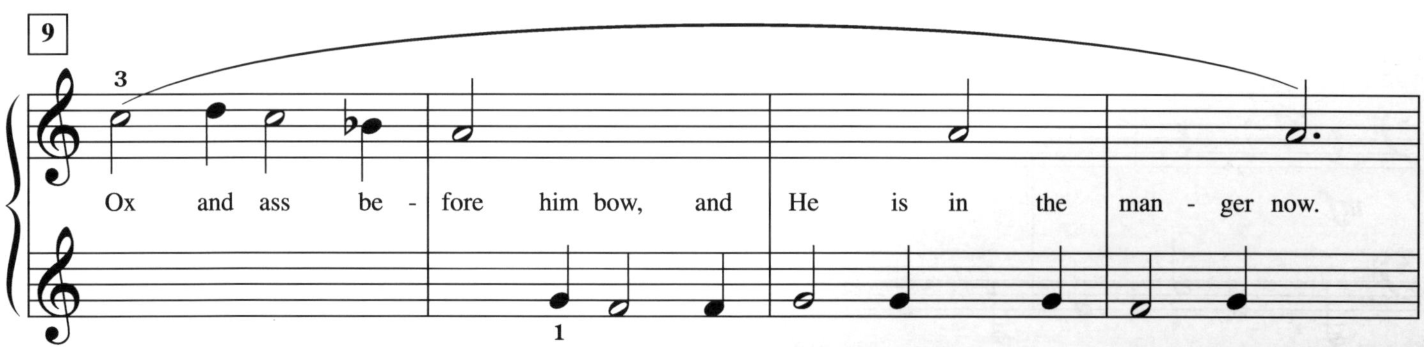

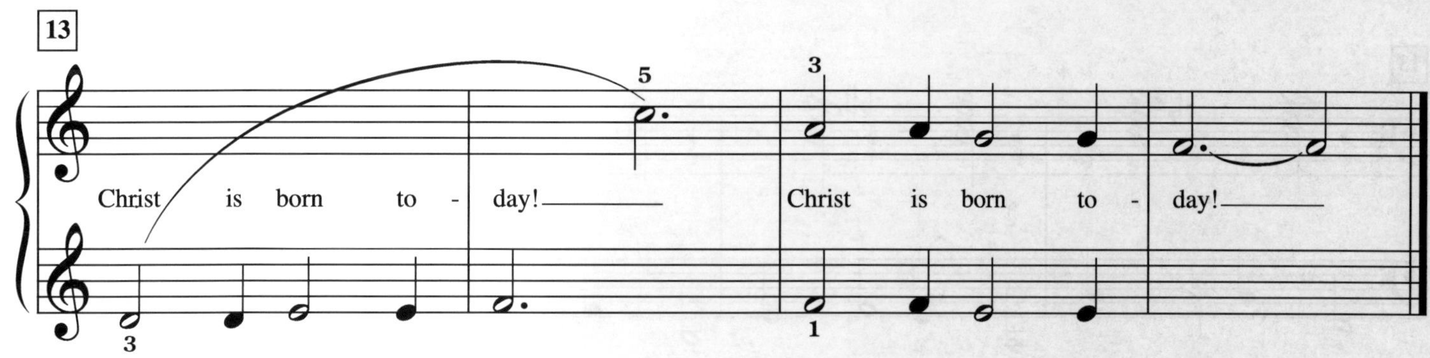

Toyland

Words by Glen MacDonough

Music by Victor Herbert

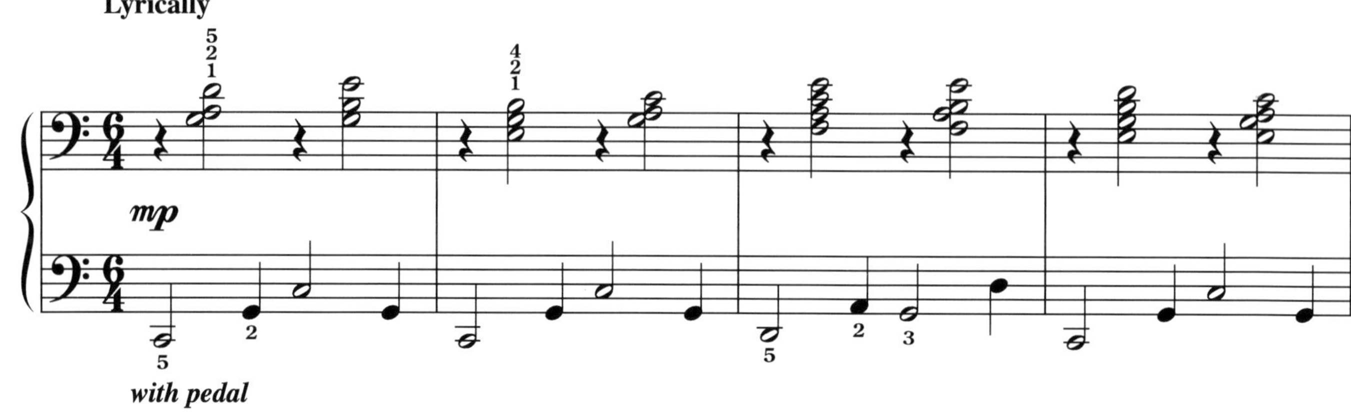

Toyland

Words by Glen MacDonough

Music by Victor Herbert

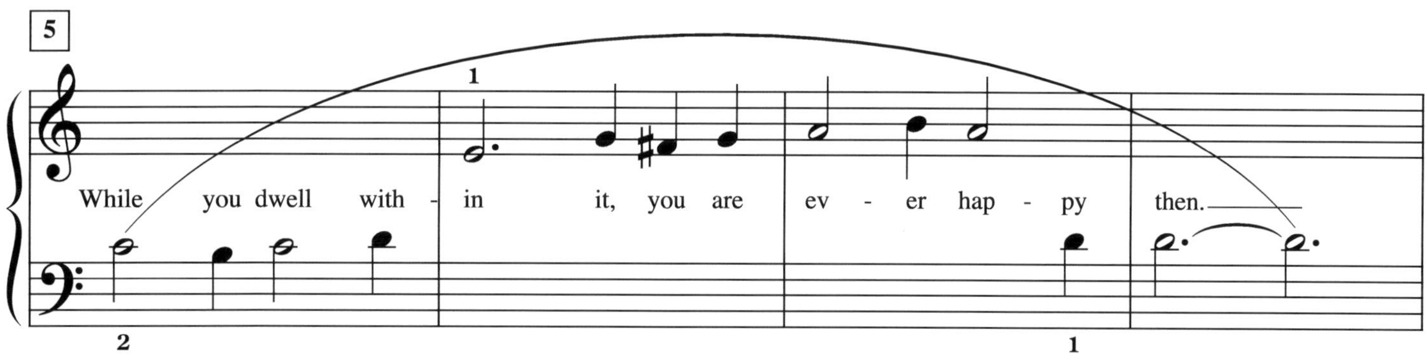

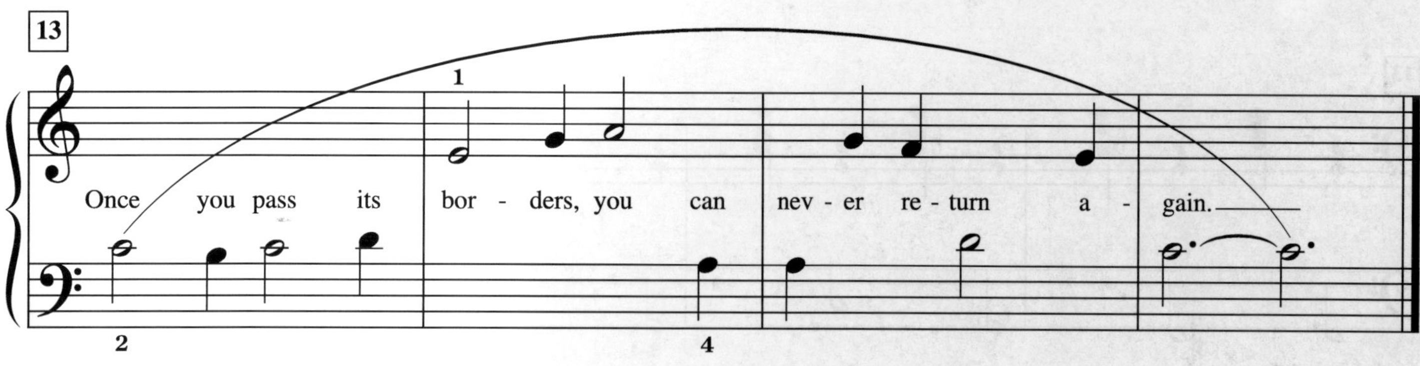

Jolly Old Saint Nicholas

Traditional

Jolly Old Saint Nicholas

Traditional

With excitement *(8va higher with duet)*

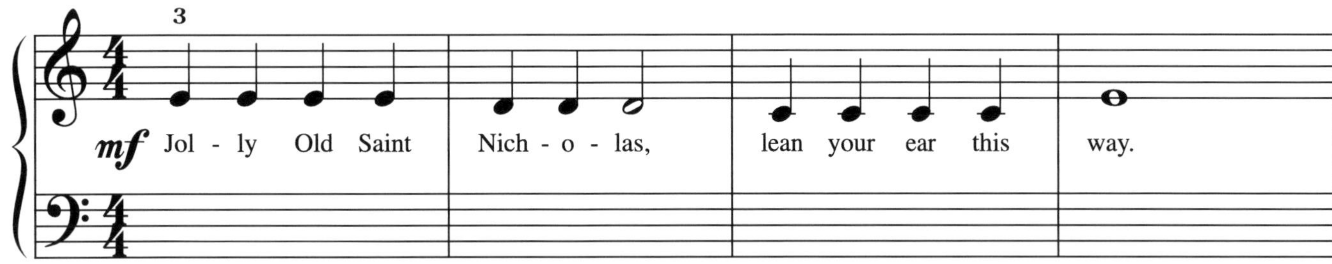

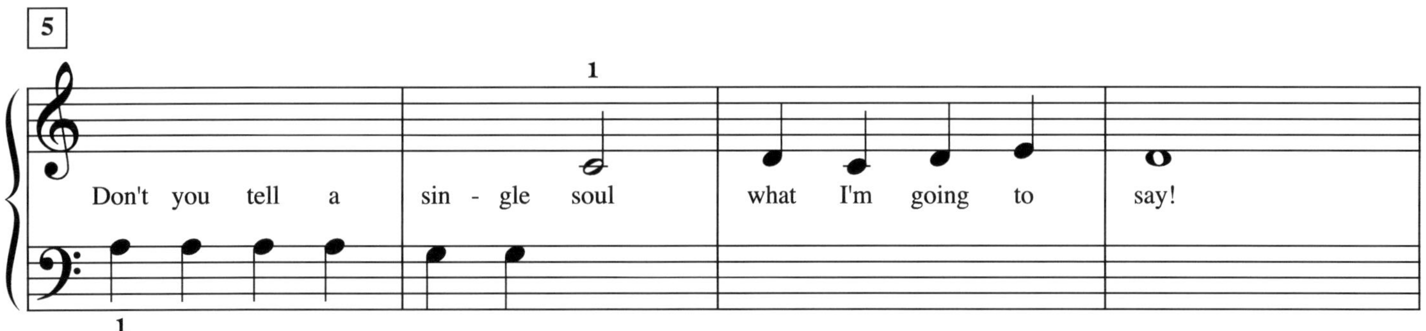

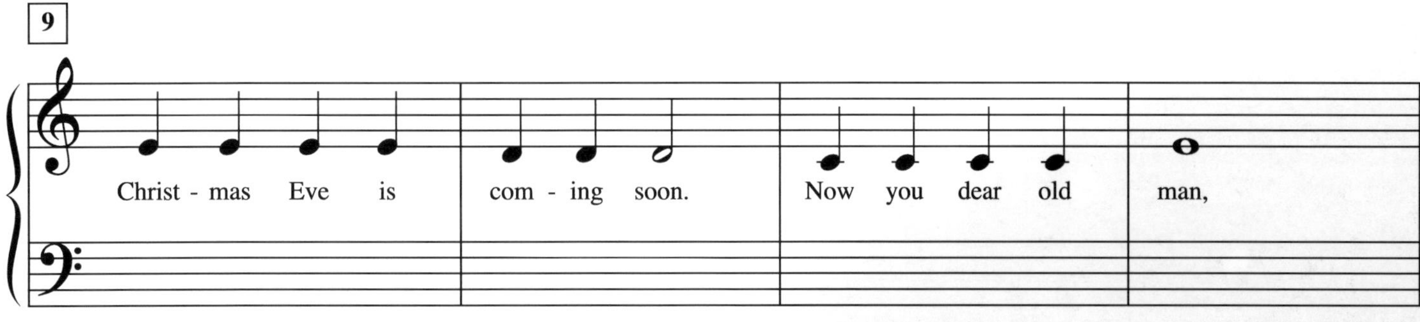